From

A to B

My 40-year Story of life with Mental Illness

by

Andy Kimmons

Disclaimer

This book has been written to provide information about my journey with a mental illness. Every effort has been made to make this book as complete and accurate as possible, but in case of any errors or out of date information, this book should be used as a guide – not as the ultimate source.

Warning: This book includes descriptions of sexual abuse and trauma, which may have a negative effect for some readers.

The purpose of this book is to educate and help others who suffer with a mental health illness as well as those who want to learn about and understand mental health.

Dedicated to my baba.

Author's Note

My name is Andy, and I am a long-time sufferer of mental health conditions.

The views in this book are mine, and mine alone, based on my life and my interpretation, and experiences, of the world I have lived in.

I hope this book will help other people struggling with mental health conditions and provide a valuable source of guidance for those on their own journey.

I also chose a larger font than normal because as someone that struggles to concentrate, especially reading, I wanted this to be as easy to read as possible.

Introduction

I think it's important to say from the start that I am not medically trained. I have no qualifications or experience in medical, mental, or any other type of education in this area. But I have over 40 years of experience as a sufferer of a mental health condition, and I wanted to share my journey in the hope it will help others.

As part of my introduction, I also wanted to point out that I am a healthy person, in that I have been cleared of any physical problems or conditions. This means that although my physical symptoms are debilitating, the cause is psychological. The reason I say this is mainly because I believe there is a misconception when it comes to mental health illnesses. A distinction is required between a physical cause or a mental cause, because depression, for example, is seen as a mental illness. But in my view depression is a physical illness, not a mental one. Why? Well, depression is a chemical imbalance of the brain. Okay, some say the evidence for this is weak, but my experience shows me this is the case, and if medication is required to correct this imbalance, it's a physical problem because the body is lacking the ability to create a certain chemical needed.

I have always argued I am not depressed, because I am not, based on my observations of those who really are. I do get down at times. I do get fed up – who doesn't? – but this does not make me depressed. It's just a word too often used in the wrong context. I will be explaining this later in the book.

This book's title, *From A to B*, is pretty much how I have always run my life, and is probably, to a large extent, why I fail at the basic level in most areas. It's how I cope, it's how I survive daily routines as well as times when I have to do things out of my routine. Consider this as blinkers, like what horses have to stop them from being scared about what's around them. They only see what's in front. So no matter the objective, be It going to the shop, having a shower, making dinner, I plan, and focus, on completing it as quick as possible.

The point of this planning and visualisation is down to keeping my brain busy, because if my brain is relaxed, every little noise, or sense, or a thought I cannot control, becomes a threat and I panic. And it's never ending. So I thought it would be a good title to explain how I live my life.

Chapter 1

The beginning of the end.

The complexities of childhood are hard to understand. The lack of experience, vocabulary and the means to articulate issues are incredibly difficult to overcome – but not impossible. This is where my problems started.

It was an ordinary school day, late in 1982. I was nine and we had moved to a new area in the South of England. Generally speaking, as the youngest of three boys, each two and half years apart from the other, I had to be boisterous to be heard by my mother and father. I was pretty confident and stood up for my friends. I remember one instance of getting into a fight with a much bigger and older kid who had been picking on my friend. Thinking back on that today makes me a little sad, because that was the boy that I was. I was punished for standing up to this bully. I had to stay with the preschool kids for the rest of the day, although I remember I actually enjoyed that. Overall I was a confident, outgoing and happy kid.

I was at my primary school, in a lesson doing art, so a lot of painting, glueing etc. As always, I got myself in a bit of a mess, so I went to get cleaned up. The school had port-a-cabins, so I had to go to the main school. It was not far, but a few steps down, and back up. As I reached the top of the stairs to the main school, I pulled the doors open to get in, my hand slipped and I went tumbling backwards down the concrete steps, bumping my head on the way down. I did lose consciousness for a period of time, but neither myself nor the school know for how long. If I were to guess, based on the time that elapsed, I would say it must have been around one to three minutes. I was gone long enough to be noticed, but not long enough for the teacher to come looking for me. I remember telling my teacher and my parents about it. But I do not recall anything else at that time.

It must have been a few days later, when I was with my mum playing at my neighbour's house, that I noticed I had a squishy head. I could actually push my fingers into my skull, and, I thought then, my brain! I spoke to my mum, and she felt it, as did my neighbour. It was enough for a doctor's visit the next day, where I was sent straight to the hospital. It seems that the fall down the steps had done more damage than expected, as I had a hematoma (bleeding between blood vessels, like a bruise) at the top of my skull. This fluid was putting pressure on my brain, but also made my head, well, squishy.

Our GP referred me to the local hospital where they diagnosed me as having a hematoma and referred me to Plymouth Children's Hospital for urgent treatment. I do not recall the treatment and I have found it difficult to find much information on it. But my mum recalls that I was in hospital in Plymouth for about a week. According to my GP's medical notes, which I requested around three years ago, my parents and teachers had seen a sizeable shift in my personality. I do not remember this myself; all I have to go on is reports by third parties. I am not sure what the shift was either, just that the boy I was before the fall was not who I was afterwards.

I should add that reading those medical notes as an adult did have a profound effect on me. I would not recommend it without having some kind of context from a parent, or older sibling. Medical notes are a third-party interpretation and as such could be misunderstood when reading them back. By this, what I mean is that, due to being young, my parents had to interpret my actions, then relay this to my GP, who in turn interpreted it in writing. What comes out is, in my case, felt like the worst case possible. It was clear reading my notes that my parents struggled with me, and they did ask for help, but it seems the help they needed was wrongly interpreted by the 'experts', because they had been looking in the wrong place.

My actions and self had not changed because of my head injury, or because I was looking for attention, it was because I was frightened of the world I now lived in. Whether or not the bump on my head had somehow made this worse nobody knows, but core to my actions and self was fear. When I spoke to my parents about these notes, and more recent hospital notes, they still recall the change from when I was a child, and being pushed in every direction ending up in the wrong place. But I do believe they did all they could at the time, and that they themselves wish they had tried harder, and helped me more. Hindsight… such as it is.

In a bid to try to understand if the fall had done any damage, months after the operation I went for a series of tests, both at Plymouth and our local hospital. However, they did not show any signs of lasting brain trauma that could account for this personality change. So I was sent to a child psychiatrist and several psychologists to find out if anything could explain the change. They didn't actually find any concrete reason or explanation either. I guess that because there had been no reason to do these tests before the accident, there was no real way of showing what change had occurred, or even if any change occurred at all. Other people saw the change in me, and their testimony encouraged the doctors to run the tests to begin with. Did I change, or did everyone's view of me change because I had an accident that could have been prevented, and this influenced their perception of me? I do not recall feeling any change in myself though, but clearly my temper was more prominent, and I started to struggle with retaining information, understanding what I was reading, and reading itself. My parents felt my personality had numbed, become cloudy – perhaps that would be a better explanation. But again there is no real evidence as to why.

What is clear from what others saw, is that I was not the same person I was, and this showed not just in my personality, but also in my school work. Because of this, it was concluded that I might have some brain damage, albeit small and medically insignificant. But I must stress that the conclusion had no real evidence behind it, it was just a possible reason for the change.

Already, then, before I was even ten years old, people had two views of me as a person (that is, they had seen two versions of my personality), but with no real evidence as to why or how this had come about.

This was the start of my journey. A simple bump on the head that altered my life course, and from here things only get worse!

Chapter 2

The second trauma.

Within twelve months of my head injury, an incident happened that caused me a different trauma.

I do not want to dwell on the specifics, because I do not believe they are relevant to this book. Trauma to one person could be water off a duck's back to another, and for another it could be near death. It's all a matter of optics. The trauma I went through does not make the trauma of anyone else more or less significant, which is my point.

What is important is the way it was dealt with, rather than what caused it. Terrible things happen to people all the time, currently unavoidable although I wish it was. To make sense of this, first, what is trauma, and, more importantly, what is childhood trauma and how is that different to any other type of trauma?

From my research over the years I have learned it's all to do with neural pathways. Pathways are how the brain operates, and changing these pathways can be much more difficult than creating them. As a child, you create many more pathways than you do as an adult. This is because your experiences, perceptions, intuitions, interactions and reactions are new. This means that although a trauma can be horrific, the pathways are formed from a blank canvas, and it could be seen as normal, even though the experiences are far from normal. Prolonged abuse can feel like normal behaviour, for example. So child abuse victims would require much support to create new pathways.

This is why the trauma, the physical experience of it, that I suffered is not as important as my mental reactions to it, and this is why I think delving into mine is not helpful, as it's all about perception and the individual.

This accords nicely with my belief that just because you have been through a similar experience and had no lasting effects, as a result, that does not mean others wouldn't. And this does not mean that because you didn't have a mental breakdown, you are either stronger or weaker in any way. It just means you had pathways in place that allowed you to understand the situation better, and an awareness of what is normal.

It could be that you had more support as a child, perhaps the help I wish I had had, but didn't. It's important to see the bigger picture, and that not everything is clear-cut. You truly need to delve into someone's life and circumstances before making rash assumptions and judgements. I believe this is the most important thing to grasp: that what matters is not what happened, but how a person deals with it. So, on to my trauma...

I grew up with loving parents in nice neighbourhoods where there was no crime, so I had no reason not to trust people, and no reason to think anyone would do me harm, no matter where I was. I was a polite child, but I was immature. This was touched on in my experiences with both the child psychiatrist and neurological consultant from the fall I had before.

This changed just after my tenth birthday, when somebody did want to do me harm. It could have resulted in my rape and murder. But, as we managed to escape one attempt, we were then being chased down again, which resulted in my friend being caught and assaulted, but with us then finally escaping. This whole ordeal lasted less than 20 minutes. So it was a bad experience, but what came out of it was twofold. First, I felt that I hadn't been listened to, because I had wanted to dive over a fence off the road into a field whilst being chased down. I knew another gate was on the opposite side of the field we could have jumped into closer to home; we might have avoided the situation had we gone that way. Hindsight notwithstanding, I felt we could both have been unscathed to the degree I was. Of course it could have been worse, who knows. The point was I had a plan to get away, but it was not taken.

Second, the perpetrator gave me a warning, having been the main one face to face I knew what they looked like, and they saw me. The warning was that if I went to the police, they would find me and kill me. As I escaped his clutches and my friend didn't, the more I tried to move away, the more my friend was being hurt. This meant I saw everything in detail, and my actions seemed to have a negative effect. This formed the feeling that people are not to be trusted, and my actions have consequences. I was only a child, so my experiences of life up till then had been very limited.

From this experience I came away with the strong perception that not all people are good, and some will harm me, and that death at the hand of another is a strong possibility . Everything I had experienced before was now in question. I also developed a strong feeling of self-control and would act on my feelings, meaning I would go in my own direction and not follow others, but more than that, if others didn't follow me, I would simply leave them behind. My judgement had been severely compromised. Where I used to feel safe around people, I now felt unsafe and vulnerable, and I didn’t trust anyone I met from this moment on.

After these experiences, I had a suspicious feeling towards all others, and I felt my way was better, no matter what. The latter was a very deep feeling, and I did blame my friend for a long time for not trusting in my escape plan. More of this came into play in later life, which explains further failings in my life.

Once he let my friend go we ran first to my house, but nobody was home. We then ran to my friend's house and nobody was there either. So we went to another friend's house, as we knew his dad was a policeman. Our friend's mother called the police and our parents for us. After interviews and the police investigation, which lasted around six weeks, the person was caught. From the time it happened until the time he had been caught I was still very nervous and felt very uneasy and unsafe. I didn't want to go out to play and I always stayed close to my brothers or my father. There were times I could not sleep without my mum holding my hand. Again, my personality and behaviour shifted: not only was I not the boy I had been, now yet another new side of me had established itself.

My behaviour, which was evolving still with recent events, was not so much blamed by others around me on my fears, but still on my head injury. Although I had the operation and recovered, I continued to evolve within my personality, but now with fear entwined. This new experience only complicated my feelings, and how I understood and processed them. But my behaviour, lack of concentration at school and pretty much everything else were blamed on my fall, and not on what is now known as Post Traumatic

Stress Disorder (PTSD). Although I felt my friend and I were lucky not to be dead in a ditch somewhere, I was too young to really recognise this. I do remember my dad taking our dog for a walk where this incident first took place, and he walked the full length of the lane, which was a dead end, to a stream and wooded area. On his return, it was my dad who said how lucky we had been to outmanoeuvre the perpetrator, and not go down that road as asked. These reinforced my new perspective on life and people in general.

I only started to feel better once I knew he had been caught, taken to court and imprisoned. I think it should be noted that much of this is down to memory, and medical notes thus far. I still don't remember noticing a change in my behaviour and personality, but I didn't trust people at all; I clearly remember that.

Knowing the perpetrator was off the streets and the risk to my life had subsided did allow me some freedoms. What this didn't do was change my behaviour. I was never again the boy I used to be, and whether it was the bump on the head, the attack, or both, I was changed for life. But I was able to try to live again, and have fun again albeit guarded.

This is, however, childhood trauma. I was exposed to a dangerous situation which I witnessed first-hand. My feelings, the sounds and smells of that moment had been locked in my mind. I understood the fear and that my brain now associated all my senses with it. This is what I mean by pathways, or more to the point, neural pathways. It is this association that makes my body feel vulnerable when it comes to my conscious mind. The pathways follow how they've been mapped, leading to fear, feeling unsafe, and finally, panic.

The paths lead on from panic to my nervous system where my body operates on the assumption something bad, even life-threatening, is going to happen. It matters not that I am in a safe place at the time, locked in my house or in my car. I am actually not in any danger, but my brain is taken on a journey and the emotions associated with it follow that path until the end. Once my nervous system has the instruction, it acts how it should: self-preservation until the end, expecting murder and death. For me, even today, this whole process can happen within five minutes from the point of feeling vulnerable. What sets it off is what I am still trying to learn and manage. After 30 years I still don't have it nailed down. I call this an episode, and I can have it any time, anywhere.

This was how my pathways took shape, but others could have a different route, and end in a different place.

Violence, self-harm, sobbing, physical pain, headaches, or just being completely switched off from the world. The point is you cannot function, everything stops while your brain travels the pathways until the end. Of course the trick is to re-map these pathways as quick as possible.

Chapter 3

A trauma returned.

This chapter is a little blurry when it comes to the timeline, as no records actually exist for what happened. But it was a defining moment in my life, and one that changed me more than anyone could ever have expected.

As a child, I used to stand up to people without fear, but my life was very different in secondary school after the two physical and emotional incidents I had lived through. Constantly being bullied and mistreated was not what I would call a happy time. In fact, I was very unhappy in secondary school. I think other children could sense my fear, and my anxiety about life in general, and capitalised on this, making me an easy victim of bullying. I was strong enough, but too afraid to fight back. I think as a child who had seen how short life could be, any type of threat was a threat to life itself, with no room in the middle. This has stayed with me throughout my life, even up to today.

So life was already hard for me, and I was unhappy away from home. Home was my castle, my safe place from bullies and the outside world, but my feeling of safety was short-lived. I am not sure how old I was, but around twelve, when one day I came home to find my mum waiting for me. 'Andy', she said, 'I have some news, and somebody is coming to explain it to you.'

It turned out the perpetrator of my attack had been released from prison, and on parole and now working out community service. What was a greater shock was that this service was in the next village from me, less than five minutes away. I remember the day like it was yesterday. I remember the feelings of anger, fear, more anger and more fear. I slammed my school bag down and shouted, "Why, how, when?' Nobody could change the way I felt. Being let out was bad enough, but for the authorities to give him community service so close to his victims was unfathomable. It was horrific. I felt my knees buckle and I knew my days were numbered. He was going to make good on his promise, and he had been helped to follow through by being so close to me. This was a breaking point for me. I feel it now when writing about it. These are the same emotions, and feelings I feel today when I step out of my routine.

The police officer who first dealt with the attack, who was now a detective, came to the house to explain things to my parents and me. They assured me that they would be moving him out of the area. They had seen him, making it clear he was not to go near me, ask about me, or look for me. They gave a special number to my parents and said they should call it if anything happened. For me, however, the mental break had already occurred. My entire life was now about self-preservation. How could I feel safe? What could I do to make sure I survived? A new me was born, yet again, and everything just got worse.

Reflecting on the last few chapters I've written, I had, in the space of only a few years – and these are young, impressionable years – experienced three instances of massive change in behaviour and personality. I have a daughter now, and I cannot imagine how she would deal with such experiences and the changes in perception that resulted. And she is older than I was then.

Despite the lost opportunities to help me before, the next ten years of my life are what defined me. The person I am today, I am because I was screaming for help, and all everyone did is blame the bump on my head. They just didn't take seriously how the attack impacted me, or how my experiences since had only reinforced my already bleak perceptions of life. The day I found out the perpetrator was out of prison was truly the day of change for me. Even if I could not take all three experiences back, but just had another go at that day, I believe I could still change my path. But hindsight is not a luxury. This was the crunch point: he was out, close by, and he would be able to act upon the vow he made. I felt powerless.

As it turned out, and as far as I was aware, I never saw the person again for many years. He never came near me while I was growing up, and didn't try to kill me. But that didn't matter. The thought of it was enough to put my family through the wringer several times over. It was never deliberate; it was a mindset forced onto me. The neural pathways formed in the much earlier attack were strongly reinforced. I was in clear and present danger and the only person I could rely on was myself. After all, what was also cemented in me was that I should follow my own instincts, because as far as I was concerned, I wouldn't have been in the place I was if I had followed them before, and jumped that fence.

From the day I knew he had been released, it was a case of locking everything down, and trusting nobody. One of the main reasons I couldn't trust anyone was because my mind had, over time, blocked out his face. To this day I have forgotten what he looked like. The last time I remember seeing him, and what he looked like, was in court. Since that day, the face has always been blank. So being unable to recognise him meant I couldn't trust anyone new that came into my life who was male. I also kept a lot of personal information secret. One of the early memories from the attack was my fear that someone might know him, and information travels. So I kept my home and age secret, or just made up stuff so nobody could connect the dots.

When I came home from school, I used to lock myself in, and would prevent others from getting in, including my family, until I saw them in the window. Being an adult now I can see how that infuriated my parents, in that they were stopped from entering their own house, but again, it was a mindset. I didn't feel safe, not even in my castle. This had always been a safe space for me, but having him do community service so close by made me uneasy. It felt like there was a reason he was there, and he must have known where I lived.

Alongside this, I was getting wiser about the world around me. Listening to the news, I recall several murders being reported and how in one of these murders the perpetrator had climbed a ladder to the first floor and got in through the window. This was paranoia, but at the time, and for several years, the threat and the ability seemed so plausible I had to do everything I could to protect myself.

One might imagine with time passing, all this would get easier. It never did. The more awareness I had of the world, the greater the realisation of what was possible, the more nervous about life I became, and especially frightened of other people. I remember my mum telling me I would not sleep without her sitting beside me on my bed. She only left when I was asleep, and this was a regular occurrence. This was in my teens.

Although my nerves were shot, I do not recall ever having episodes, like I would in later life. I do not recall the fear being so great I would have panic attacks. And I could not find anything about any of this in my notes. But I did have behaviour problems, mostly at school. I found it very difficult to concentrate and being bullied and misunderstood took its toll on me.

But what frustrated me more, is that I was not helped, or not helped enough. Everything went back to the bump on my head, even though with several tests undertaken there was no evidence of permanent brain damage. This was the early 1990s, and PTSD was not yet a diagnosed condition. That said, it was known about, but only under the name 'Shell Shock'. Another name for the same thing, but it was believed to be associated with extreme, stressful situations, such as war. But still, I was eating, my digestion seemed to function normally, like the rest of my family, and I had no record of the issues I have now.

At the end of this chapter, I was still a very young teenager who had undergone three experiences that altered my personality, behaviour and my perception of my environment. I was at that point a very complicated young person in whom the blurred lines from these experiences met and crossed.

Mental trauma is never just one thing, the emotions, feelings, and symptoms of it are fluid. Like a wave that constantly moves, and grows in size, my thinking and interpretations of my surroundings would also move, and grow.

The final twist in my reason for being the person I am is what comes next.

Chapter 4

The twist of fate.

I was in my late teens. I had finished school and had had a few jobs, but none that lasted and none that I enjoyed. Still under constant stress and fear, I was reluctant, but did go out into the world. I still had feelings of distrust and felt closer to women than I did to men, especially mistrusting those I didn't know. I lied all the time, to hide the truth about my personality and identity. I didn't want to be bullied and I needed my privacy. It actually became a habit, and one I was good at. Another dreadful experience I had around that time had far-reaching and long-lasting implications.

I do not recall the exact circumstances, but I was very poorly for around five days, being sick, suffering from diarrhoea and basically feeling terrible. Unable to leave my bed or keep any food or drink down made me very vulnerable. It wasn't until I was able to get to the GP and provide samples it was found I had gastroenteritis.

Although it took some time to get over the virus, it seemed to take much longer to get over the experience. I had several weeks of episodes when symptoms would return, and I was fearful of being ill again. I already had a pattern of being picky with food, but this was a completely new thing. My fear of vulnerability, worrying I wouldn't be able to escape if someone came after me because I was bedridden for so long, was mixed up with my other anxieties from previous traumatic experiences, and a new link had formed between the digestive and psychological symptoms.

During this period of my life, I was often at the doctor's. I couldn't understand why I was having so many tummy issues and why I felt sick. My fear of going outside only increased. It made no sense that I was feeling the way I did, and I will admit it was getting me down. I was made to think it was me being lazy, and I was making it all up. When you are young, and if, as in my case, you've had a poor education, it is tough to articulate what is happening and how you're feeling. I realise this now, but at the time it felt like nobody cared, and that I was more of a problem than anything else. But I did always try to be a help, because that is one trait that has never left me. I always try.

Over the next several years, I attempted to take my own life. I no longer wanted to live the way I was or feel the way I did. Finally I expressed this to a caring female doctor, and I was given instructions to see a counsellor on a weekly basis, and medications to make me 'feel' better. I do not want to dwell on suicide, nor my attempts. A big part of wanting to share this story is to show that my life would have stopped here, had I succeeded. Yes, my life has been painful, physically and emotionally, but in reality, whose life hasn't, in one way or another?

But I failed, and the fact I carried on shows a lot of positives. Not understood back then, perhaps not understood twenty years ago, looking back at the bigger picture demonstrates what benefit I have brought to my own life, and to others' lives; what ripples through time my size 11 feet have made, and the impact I've had on others.

When I was young, I felt that I could only depend on myself. I trusted only myself and I feared everyone. Opening up was, and is, challenging for me and I think I never really have, until now. From my experience to date, I formed the opinion that nobody really understood me, nor the way I think or the way I perceive others. Even if I talked to them honestly, as a child, it was like I was talking in a foreign language. I was speaking, and they heard me, but never understood me. I have felt much like this my entire life.

Because of this I actually found counselling awkward, but I guess that is because I never really opened up to it. I was looking for reasons why my body was acting the way it was, and a cure. I thought for a very long time something was physically wrong with me. And to this day I think there is a degree of truth in that. But back then, it was new, and I was afraid of life, as much as of death. And now I was afraid I was seriously ill too, because of the constant nausea, and actually being sick. Whereas now my condition has evolved into pain and diarrhoea, and vomiting in extreme panic attacks, back then it was constant pain and being sick all the time. I was physically vomiting a lot, especially when I had to do things where I felt vulnerable, which was pretty much all the time, to be honest.

Needless to say, counselling was not helpful. I was going for test after test to try to find out what the issue was, how the pain had come about, and whether it was related to what I was eating. So just like today, I was testing everything to find out if I had an allergy or intolerance to any food type. I wrote a diary for several weeks, hoping to find a pattern. As it happens, no pattern was seen, that is, not relating to my intake of food. While having these tests alongside counselling, I was not really getting any closer as to the reasons why. And because of this, it turned into a fantasy. By this I mean it was thought

I was making it up, either for attention or to get out of doing any type of work.

I should point out that a lot of people do get help by seeing counsellors, but I do think there are cases where an individual has a complex case, and the root of the problem is difficult to find. I am such a case. Remembering what we talked about, it seems the counselling was focused more on my day-to-day issues and my resentment of the many that I felt put me there, rather than on trying to discover the root causes.

Over my lifetime I have had several further attempts at counselling, the last back in 2017. None of the counselling I have had has ever helped cure me. In that most recent treatment, I suppose I could say I looked at things slightly differently in that I always saw my physical pain as the cause, and the mental panic as the symptom. But based on this therapy, it seems it's the other way around. I cannot wrap my head around this. The explanation I was given for why I was having these episodes, and when I was having them, didn't make much sense. Basically, I was doing it to myself. My trigger was a mixture of emotions that, when combined, caused physical pain, resulting in diarrhoea, sickness and depression. I simply do not buy that explanation, though. I do get weak, physically and mentally, after an episode, and the experience is exhausting, which makes me a bit fed up, but not depressed. Why I would cause myself pain deliberately is beyond my understanding.

Having had many different types of counselling such as Cognitive Behavioural Therapy (CBT), which have never resolved the issue, means I am no better off than when I was a teenager.

I recall a CBT session where I had an episode in front of the counsellor due to a stressful phone call. It was good timing in a way because here the counsellor could actually see what the CBT was meant to prevent. Instead, whilst panicking and feeling very poorly and vulnerable, she said she couldn't help me and that CBT was not the answer. I do remember her face of shock, and clear she had no idea how to help me.

I do not have any evidence from before the gastroenteritis of being physically sick, and diarrhoea. So it did have a profound impact. Today many people that suffer from IBS (Irritable Bowel Syndrome) had gastroenteritis in their past. Those that do suffer from IBS have a massive range of triggers from diet, stress, or other physical causes.

I should probably point out that IBS is a nonsensical phrase that actually means very little to those that suffer. It provides no reason for the discomfort it can cause, even after a number of tests. It seems to be the goto conclusion when nothing else is found. Part of this conclusion is “at least it's not serious”! That maybe, but the symptoms some people have are horrendous and feels very serious to those that have to deal with it day in, day out.

So it is difficult to know how my episodes really started, only that the four experiences I had did, in various ways, have some degree of impact.

But to me clearly counselling does not help everyone.

Chapter 5

Relations and relationships

A relationship is formed with every contact a person has, whether with another person, object or animal. First impressions count, but when you have no trust at all, it's not just about the first impression, it's a never-ending questioning. I have no trust in people, and throughout my life I have found evidence that demonstrates to me why people do not deserve it. My problem is that I look at things in black and white. No grey exists in my world of relationships and when a glimpse of it shows itself, I just want to run away. The harsh reality is, I am alone today because I am standing in my own way.

I had my first sexual experience around

the age of seventeen. I think it is important to set the scene for this part of my life. I was what you could call a lost soul. I had a job under YTS (Youth Training Scheme) where I worked in a garage as a back office clerk. I was immature in nature with no real education to speak of. My social skills had become awkward and so I had no friends. All I had was my insecurities outside and feeling lonely and misunderstood inside. I was craving for some kind of attention from anyone.

I was interested in girls, but I had no way of communicating with them and with no self-worth myself I had no confidence to even try. It should be said I was a pretty good-looking lad, just so long as you didn't talk to me, and I wouldn't talk back.

Around this time one of my brother's friends befriended me. He was older, and I knew him and his family well. I do not remember how it happened, but involved sexual acts on him. It was, as I remember, always him first, and initially he never did anything to me. But because I did this, I had a friend. This carried on and then he started to touch me. I didn't really resist and there was no physical force to any of it. I guess at the time it felt normal, perhaps that was what people did, based on experiences I have had to date. If I refused, he would be cold and distant, and I would not hear from him for a few weeks. He would blank me in passing and I suppose I didn't exist for him. But he would come back and try again, and if I accepted, he would be friendly again. I knew I was not gay, I didn't particularly enjoy the acts, but the friendship I did. Not being alone was nice.

This only went on for a few months, until he wanted me to do more than I was willing, and I guess he gave up.

Our meetings stopped and I went back to being alone. But because I thought this was normal behaviour among male friends, I met up with an old friend from school and tried to do the same. Clearly, it was a mistake and I never saw him again after that. That hurt me, because he was actually someone who hadn't bullied me in school, and we used to get on really well. But I blew it.

It is probably worth explaining that this 'normal behaviour among males' had already been acknowledged when a much older man that used to work in a local petrol station exposed himself to me, asking me to touch him, or as he put it, help him. I didn't help him, and I left pretty swiftly. Also the sexual nature of the attack I witnessed when I was nine. So I guess in hindsight I can see why what my brother's friend was asking wasn't so odd to me, as this particular incident had happened when I was around sixteen.

This experience actually taught me a valuable lesson, and one I would not repeat. It also further cemented the view of life I already had, that people are mean and selfish and can't be trusted. Even more than that, it reinforced my feeling of being seen as weak, and someone who was easily taken advantage of. This issue of vulnerability really had, and still has, a massive impact on my life. How I was seen really became a focus for me and I knew I had to change. I just didn't know how.

My next sexual encounter was when I was twenty. It was with a girl I met at college, where I was studying hotel management as a mature student. Not having the required social skills, I found college very challenging and difficult to navigate. I still had my issues and suffered from my vulnerabilities. But being older, starting at nineteen years of age in a college with seventeen-year olds, I found getting girlfriends to be pretty easy, so I capitalised on this to make up for lost time.

Another change I had in my life at the time was that I finally made a friend, actually someone I had known since primary school. He was a real friend too, and he helped me so much more than he ever realised, especially in becoming more mature and understanding social signals. I should add that, as with every relationship, I screwed that up too by borrowing money with no way of paying it back, followed by getting caught up in other relationships and I guess ignoring him. This is one part of my life I have a huge amount of regret over. Relationships, no matter what type, are difficult for me to understand.

Around the age of twenty-three I found my first true love. This was a feeling I hadn't felt before, not to this degree of intensity. Looking back, I think it was because she was out of my league. She was bright, funny, caring, beautiful and she liked me. We met while working for a holiday camp in North Devon, and then moved around the country together doing different jobs. We even got engaged. But I was young, and I still had my vulnerabilities and issues, even though I had been managing to mask them well. It was on the eve of us moving into our new place together that I had a wobble. I had a panic attack and I told her I had doubts about getting married. To this day I cannot recall what brought it on, whether it was a test of trust, or I really just didn't want to get married. By the next day we had broken up and she was on her way home, 300 miles away.

I was devastated. Words cannot express the anger I felt at myself for speaking out, nor my feeling of loss. But by the end of that day I had a home I could no longer afford to move into, with new household items, no job to pay for it all, and I was 300 miles away from the girl I loved. Me and my big mouth.

I was struggling to let go, trying so very hard to find a way back to her. I recall the time well, and the hardships I faced, not just emotionally, but physically. I ended up back in a bedsit living alone, lost and vulnerable.

Based on these new experiences, and building on my life experiences thus far, I did develop a path I would follow regardless. Looking back, it was selfish, but I remember that at the time I had one real guide in life, and that was my instinct. It was a groove through life I was locked into and people either followed it or didn't and drifted away. I know people assumed this was controlling and that is one thing I hate to be called. I do not see it as controlling, I

am not forcing anyone to follow me, but I feel compelled to stick to my path and not be adventurous and deviate. After all, I had this belief that following my instinct could prevent me from ill-fated endings. I knew I could trust it to save me as, in my mind at least, it had so far. I had never expected to stay alive this long, as I grew up thinking my days were numbered from the age of ten.
Am I alive because I have always followed my instincts? It was, and is, my belief it was. The reason we have instincts is our minds self-preservation. I do accept though that at times they can be wrong.

Despite this, I think over the years this attitude has had a profound impact, and a major part of this was my subtle test. Because I just didn't trust people, even if I loved them, I couldn't find it in me to think anyone would want to be with me when I felt broken so often and was ill so much. I wanted to give them the opportunity to leave. By this I mean I would say something so they would start to question my true feelings for them, which in my head meant they would question their feelings for me. I never meant what I said, and those who knew me the longest knew this. It was designed only as a method of ensuring I could trust, or that the trust I had given was safe. It also gave them an easy out. I wanted to create a situation where they had a valid reason to end things, should they choose, so the fault would be mine and they could leave without blame being allocated to them. In hindsight, I guess this was a pitiful gesture, but at the time it was important to feel assured. I have never been interested in drama and wanted to avoid it at all costs.

I think this distrust I have is on a scale so large that now I cannot overcome it. The experiences I have had, the heartbreaks (and I have had a few) and fear of having to steer away from my own path because of someone else, like I have in the past, are too much.

However, this shouldn't stop others that suffer from trying to find that someone special. The experiences you gain from it can be life-changing. Yes, relationships can be good, or bad, but that's life, and although you may see things differently because you suffer from a mental illness shouldn't mean you should always be isolated. Remember the ripples: you're not just helping yourself, but others too.

What I have found personally is that I seem to be happier on my own. I do not crave any type of intimate relationship. In fact it probably scares me whenever I do think about it. I can follow my own path, and when I do have episodes, I can deal with them without the fear or stress of how it may affect others.

I find myself now a single parent, and have been for over eleven years. I suppose when my daughter has left home to run her own life, I will be alone again, and perhaps I will find a companion and we will grow old together. Maybe my symptoms will have changed again, perhaps I will have found medication that helps, or a treatment that fixes my condition.

Only time will tell. I can say that without my daughter I would have probably returned to old ways with drink. She has given me a motivation that I would never have had otherwise, and the will to live and fight the good fight. There really is no telling how I would have turned out, or even if I would still be on this earth, without this gift. Perhaps this is my role in life, as I feel we all have a purpose in life.

Chapter 6

Periods of Relief

I have had periods of my life where things seemed to be working out. However, these were always short-lived, and I needed the help of either illegal drugs or alcohol to feel OK. I have never been able to live in the same way with prescribed medication or any type of therapy. I think there is a lot to be said about that.

The mind is a complex component of the body, which links everything together. Mental illness, much like any addiction, is also a mind game. The person has to want to get better; a lot of willpower is needed to beat the symptoms and develop mental strength. Support for this is vital, but the will to get better and the preparation for the hard work needed to succeed are just as important to beat the debilitating effects.

For me, the fact I could function better using illegal drugs or alcohol proves that the brain is an obstacle to itself, and if you can remove this obstacle it will function as it should. The downside to this is that it's short-lived, and prolonging or increasing the substance abuse only leads to further medical, mental and social issues. This only masks the problem, and doesn't resolve it; it could even lead to a person's demise in unintended ways. This of course complicates treatment, which will inevitably take longer to manage, and perhaps even cure, the problem.

There is of course much more help out there today than back when I started struggling, but even today I see children fall through the gaps. I can see a path of abuse on their horizon, and I feel powerless to help. For someone who has suffered, the thought of others going through it and being powerless to help is extremely hard, even soul-destroying at times. But it's not just that; I still find it difficult to manage myself, and I just don't have the confidence to go out, but I also have a fear of meddling or being seen as putting my nose in where it's not wanted. My own social awkwardness would make this worse while I try to communicate my concerns and offer help by signposting. It could also make it worse for the child, as perhaps they are not ready. It's a difficult situation to be in.

Having a child myself who has gone through primary, and is now in secondary education, I see the stresses of school life have not changed that much from when I was that age. But the world has changed, and I fear education, itself, has not moved with the times, especially not when it comes to mental health. However, I also think that ultimately this issue is not for our educators to deal with; it's the parents' job. Teachers have enough to do without being therapists as well. I truly believe teachers should only teach, and it's parents that need to make sure the child is ready and able to learn. And if the child is not, don't just label them with useless acronyms and send them on their way. Get outside help, and as early as possible.

I say this because falling for drugs or alcohol abuse is so easy today, as it is an easy fix for the suffering person, regardless of age. It is a short-term fix, yet has lasting consequences, with the ability to break families apart as well as having an unwanted social impact. It can mask real underlying problems that need to be resolved and understood, and need to have processes put in place to help manage them.

There are no winners here, except those who profit from it. These are people that see just the numbers and not real people. They are indifferent to those who suffer and while they can turn a profit in the market, alcohol and illegal drugs will always be available. I am not suggesting we make alcohol illegal. Drugs are illegal, yet you can buy them on most streets if you know where to look. No, we need to focus on why there is a need for drugs, not on the response to it. This starts with educating not just children, but their parents as well. Our governments must allow parents to parent, and ensure they're not so busy they are not able to attend to their children's needs.

If we could remove the need, then drug and alcohol abuse would fade into the history books as a bygone era, but we have to make a start today to ensure that, in the future, all children have the same opportunities. And a good start to this is to make sure parents have the time to parent, rather than being bogged down working two or three jobs to keep the heating on and food on the table. And if parents are struggling for whatever reason, put the needs of the child first, even if that means removing them and placing them in a different environment that is supportive. Not all people are cut out to be parents, just as not all people are cut out to be lawyers or surgeons. This does not make them useless to society, it just means they have other ways to contribute. As I have said, we are all important.

I hope this gives people hope that there is always another way to help the next generation and that if a problem is recognised early enough, and the child or young person is helped, it will carry them through to a better tomorrow.

Chapter 7

Evolution of symptoms.

It is clear to me that the symptoms I started with when these traumas happened to me are not the same as what I am going through now. There are definitely similarities and a few identical underlying symptoms, but for the most part, they manifest differently. A lot of this is down to the many different types of diagnoses I have had, and the medications I have been given, but also, perhaps to a greater extent, my experience of life itself. I have had many knocks along the way, as we all do. Like so many, I have managed to dust myself off and try to move forward. But each knock adjusted my direction when it comes to how I interpret life and how I perceive interactions with others, and these changes must have affected my symptoms.

With the combination of life experience, diagnosis and medication over the years, I honestly find this an integral part of my life that others can learn from. Once you're on a path dealing with mental illness, the complexities only become more complex, more blurred to the point of becoming lost. I cannot stress enough how important it is that when we see children struggling we act quickly, but even more importantly, give them a correct diagnosis. One reason for writing this book is to shed light on this often unseen side effect: a wrong diagnosis then leads to backtracking, making it difficult for a child to understand the effects of different treatments in close succession. If we think about it, we are evolving, learning and understanding at an alarming rate when we are young.

But there is only so much our brains can absorb, and too much information can harm us – something has got to give. A child's distress is not invisible: there are signs, but the person suffering may have trouble explaining it, so we need to be mindful of its possible existence. How the problems come about is of course dependent on the child and the environment they are living in, and grew up in.

The screams of those that do suffer should be heard, and acted upon, not labelled and seen as a weakness, or deliberate fault. Like any seed that grows at an odd angle, a damaged person needs help and support to right themselves. Otherwise, the direction of growth is harmful to itself, and the environment around it. This is how I see the early to middle years of my life.

Bearing in mind each child is different, the complex side effects of doing nothing are no worse than trying and getting it wrong. There might be several options that require testing before you find the right one for the person. Although I speak often of children, adults can suffer in much the same way. But in adults, it's easier to recover from any type of mental illness, unless they have carried it with them from a young age. There is no one way that fits all, and so time and patience are required. Those are things we have little of these days, but for the sake of our family and friends, we need to make time and deal with it head-on.

Another issue with evolution, especially when talking about mental health, is that the complexities can also bring about awareness of, or create new physical symptoms that, when left untreated, can cause serious life-changing conditions. These are easy to miss, so we rely on our GPs to take the time and work on solutions. But today, doctors themselves are struggling with their workload. This is why friends and families should look out for each other, and we all need to be educated on the various mental illnesses so as not to dismiss it. The screams should be heard, and it is on all of us to do our bit within our own small social circles.

It is also important for us, armed with some awareness and at least some knowledge, to foresee possible problems and not let those important to us walk down blind alleys alone. For adults, all we can do is give suggestions and advice, but for children, we need to ensure and even enforce protection. This will help because it prevents further complexities arising should things go wrong. This does not mean stopping them from trying new ideas, or different coping mechanisms in real life situations. It really means walking through it alongside them: an important distinction, as we want minds to get stronger, and this will not happen by being overprotective and sheltering our young people.

In my own experience, the slightest influence can change my triggers and the causes of panic. Whether food-related or environmental, I cannot do things I used to be fine with. Sometimes I think I can do something, only to find the benefit of doing it is outweighed by the negative impact of my symptoms, and the recovery from it.

Mental illness has, in my view, two principal causes: a physical cause, perhaps a chemical imbalance, and trauma. The former case, for the most part, can be fixed with medication. Trauma is an association, or link, of sensors, emotions and memory. Both physical and trauma-related causes can bring about physical and emotional symptoms that can be debilitating. With my own mental illness I need to point out that, as of yet, no physical causes have been found, and it does seem to be trauma-related.

So, what does this actually mean in my everyday life today? Well, I guess the first point I would make is that it is uncontrollable and unforeseeable. I can be fine one minute and a complete mess five minutes later, so I always have to be prepared for it to happen and have strategies in place for when it does. This means every part of my life is a plan, with escape routes.

The reason these plans are needed is that the symptoms are as follows. First, severe, uncontrollable panic attacks consisting of shaking, dizziness, hot and cold flushes, and headaches. This is then followed closely by bad cramps in my tummy, and these are not like trapped wind, but like a knife being twisted in the gut, eye-watering pain that forces me to keel over. This leads to my bowel being emptied completely in one go: from top to bottom the contents of my gut are forced out, and in bad episodes, I violently vomit up the contents of my stomach. When these symptoms occur, I call them episodes. They can last for anything from twenty minutes to an hour, after which I am entirely drained, sore and weak. It takes at least three days to recover, and up to ten days for a bad episode.

It is worth recounting that I cannot see the attacks coming and they are based solely on emotions. It can happen while listening to music, or watching a film or programme. Night or day, no matter where I am, an attack can come over me suddenly. I have been unable to find out which specific emotions, or a combination of more than one, are the triggers; I only know that the feeling of vulnerability is a part of it.

Chapter 8

Money: how I survived.

Due to my inconsistency when it comes to doing anything, work has always been an issue. I have tried three careers: in retail, construction, and the food and drink industry. Each time I managed to get to some type of management level quickly, but the downside of these jobs was stress and not having enough energy. Although it was easier when I was younger, that was probably only because I had help from alcohol, drugs, or both. None of my jobs lasted long-term. I always crashed and burned because my body gave up. This meant income has been very hit and miss throughout my life. This was because of my eating habits, and the link with vulnerabilities.

In terms of getting money when I was not working, which has been most of my adult life, I have received various benefits from the government. Getting on benefits is easy in this country if you are unemployed. However, if you are long-term sick, the process is painfully long, complicated and sometimes awkward. This is even the case if you have a physical disability, but it's so much harder when you have an invisible illness! How do you explain to someone that a disabling condition exists when no visible evidence proves it? This is one problem that requires solving urgently.

I think I should point out, like in any area of life, there are people who are dishonest; they just can't be arsed and want to live on benefits. However, in my experience, they are a tiny minority. The existence of benefit fraud, though, has made the obstacles for others too great. The key here is evidence.

If you have evidence from healthcare professionals that you have a health issue, then the benefit system must make it easier to access financial support. Each person must also be recognised as an individual, not just a National Insurance Number. They should be given help and support to make a difference in their community, providing there is no short or long-term harm to the individual or the community. The people I have met along my journey would be happy to do something to help the community. Stuffing envelopes, writing articles... Just because a person has a disability, visible or otherwise, does not make them useless. It makes them unsuitable for a 'normal' working life as most people understand it.

I hear the argument that people will be taken advantage of, and would be at risk of slave labour. I understand that, and processes and checks must be in place to prevent this. But life is for living, and living means contributing, whether that is half an hour or twenty hours a week. The boost it gives people to feel they're contributing is massive. But this does need to be means-tested for each individual. I honestly feel it is worth the investment from the government. I am a prime example, and although my condition and the reasons behind it are complex, the end result is the same for so many. Normal social and working environments don't always allow people with mental illnesses to achieve a decent standard of living.

However, the way the system works, it's a world of box-ticking without any real review of your case. In fact, even when you have to take your case to a tribunal, this only really scratches the surface.

The process is simple in itself. First, you get an application and send it to the benefits department, with any evidence you have from GPs or other services. The application form is pretty comprehensive. They review it and send it to an assessor. These are 'medical professionals'. You're given an appointment with one of these people, and they pretty much ask you the same questions as the form, but you have to answer them again in your own words. They tick boxes and write notes. Then the assessor's report is sent back to the benefits people with a view. The benefits people then review this report and score it against the government's criteria. If you meet those criteria, you are given the benefits. If not, your claim is denied.

My application was rejected every single time. According to the powers that be, I do not fit the minimum criteria. At this point, if you have been receiving the benefit and it's reviewed, the benefit is immediately stopped and so you have no money. You then have to ask the benefit people to reconsider the result, adding more evidence, if you have any. And every single time, this is rejected. At this point, the only option left is a tribunal: a type of court where a judge and a panel of experienced GPs and other health professionals hear your case. Again, you have to attend in person.

A judge then decides on whether your case has met the court's interpretation of the criteria and either reverses or supports the benefit people's view. This process can take nine months or more, so if you are successful, the benefit is back-dated to the application received date. For me, every time I went through this process the judge has found my health condition is supported and has reversed the benefits decision. Many disabled people have to go through this, and it's incredibly stressful.

Again, I understand there are some people who will try to make fraudulent claims. But if you have evidence that can be obtained from a GP, it's less likely to be a fraudulent claim. I have medical evidence dating back to the 1990s, including my head injury and trauma. With the number of doctors and specialists that can give evidence about my episodes, I am certainly a candidate for a long-term health condition. It's invisible at first glance, but take a closer look and you will see it. I think this goes for the massive majority of people that suffer with a type of disability.

This experience for some is too much, and they give up. They either rely on family and friends for money, try to go self-employed, or take the criminal route. In these cases it's pure desperation and their standard of life is very poor. I feel for them, the ones people say 'fall through the cracks'. These are real people; they are important to our society, and we need to support them. I find it sickening that we allow *anyone* to fall through the cracks. We know it happens, but do we cover the cracks? What do you think?

I have gone through this system many times, and it's harder each time, not just because of my health, but more the fact that nobody cares. You are a number, whether you have evidence or not. After the number, you are some boxes ticked on a piece of recycled paper. That is what being on benefits means. And with reviews every two to three years, living with that pressure and stress, as well as dealing with your symptoms and strategies to get through the day, becomes exhausting, and it all seems so pointless.

If you are fraudulent, you will be found out, they will claw their money back and rightly so. But if you are legitimate, with evidence to support your disability, it should be made easier and less stressful, with more support available. This includes support to get back into some type of work. Again, those of us with these conditions are not useless, just unable to maintain a normal working life.

Chapter 9

Is it genetics.

This is a question often asked! I would urge anyone to research it online, and use more than one source, ideally four. Then use your own experience in making a determination.

My view is that it's not. I believe mental health issues and trauma stem from environmental factors starting from the womb and throughout a person's life. I am one of three boys and I suffer because of traumatic events early in my life. My brothers do not suffer as I do. My daughter is showing signs of panic attacks in certain situations, could this be because of my genes? I do not believe it is because of my genes that she is showing those signs.

From the research you may have done, you may see there have been plenty of studies in this area, and nobody can say either way that mental illness conditions like anxiety and panic disorders are genetic. But as we grow, we do tend to copy our parents' signals. This is what I refer to when I speak of the environment. It is thought our awareness starts in the womb, a few months before birth. Once born we can then map some of these awarenesses to real-world environments and I do not think it's a stretch to say tendencies in one direction or another are formed. My personal view is that when we are born, we are a blank canvas and outside influences make us who we are, but that doesn't mean I am right, and my opinion shouldn't be taken as fact.

Playing devil's advocate, if it were the case that the causes are genetic, could this be an answer to fixing these debilitating symptoms? I pose this question because as I have said, the world needs all types of people, even the broken ones, as this helps understand the non-broken. I probably should explain I do not consider people with mental illnesses broken, but different. I consider myself broken because I have been unable to manage it. But that's just me, and I don't want to label others that way.

But what would happen if a gene is identified as the culprit in panic disorders, and that gene is removed? How would this change the person's personality, and thus their life circumstances? I say to my daughter that panic and feeling it are important because your senses are warning you about possible dangers, however small. Would I really want to remove that from her? Well, I can answer that: no! We need these feelings to keep us safe, but we also need to understand them and the environment we are in, so that we can then decide whether the panic is warranted. This is often difficult to do while you're in the middle of a panic attack.

Using our senses to navigate everyday life is so important and probably vital to our very survival. Having some way to suppress this could also lead to other issues to do with our personality in general. Perhaps it would affect the way we care for others, or even see ourselves in the world. This would then create a domino effect that makes our lives, or society in general, more difficult, but in ways we can't foresee or predict.

Basically, I do not believe removing parts of ourselves is the answer. It has to be about allowing us time to re-programme, rather than delete. What makes human life so interesting is that we are individually unique, and that together we find common grounds of tolerance within a majority. Quirks and all! This is why we, maybe you, despite the struggles you have, or see around you, are so important. Not only are our differences important, but it is vital to allow our diverse nations to understand each other better and so grow this tolerance. We do this by reaching out, listening, talking and, most of all, understanding.

Genetics may, or may not, be the reason, but if we start changing our very beings, I feel we would lose more than we gain in the long term, and it's a slippery slope from there.

Chapter 10

The problem with mental health.

From the outset, I explained that the reasons behind the symptoms are not so relevant, other than to prevent such situations in the future and protect others. When I speak of mental illness I see it as a condition of self-destruction within one's mind, whereas conditions such as depression, bipolar disorder, or schizophrenia are more to do with chemical imbalances in the brain that medication can help improve. This is not to say that those with chemical imbalances don't have the same anxieties as I do. I know some people who do suffer with both issues, which can become even more complicated.

So here is the problem: how do we differentiate between a mental health condition that is chemical-related, and one that's created through neural pathways, and so no chemical imbalance exists? This creates a challenge for us all, as I believe a great deal of the problems society has with understanding and even accepting mental illness as a real condition is the disconnect between the two.

For example, I have met people with real depression. It is heartbreaking to see how negative and withdrawn they feel. Yet, when given the right medication, some of them can completely turn this around and function in life without issue or concern. This is not, in my view, a mental condition, because the cause is a lack of something physical: in this case, a certain chemical in the brain. The psychological side of it is a symptom. Both are real, but due to the nature of the cause, in some cases depression should be seen as a physical illness.

I would suggest this goes for any illness where a physical deficiency, or even surplus, exists. As for mental illness, symptoms are in many cases just as, if not more, debilitating to live with, making understanding the physical aspects easier than the mental. But today physical illnesses are taken more seriously, and they tend to be easier to diagnose and treat.

This does not prevent mental illnesses from remaining an issue. This is part of the complexities that come with this illness. A treatment aimed at one symptom may well cause new symptoms. I was taking over twelve pills a day just to function, and I was on them for years. It was not until I realised that most of the pills I was taking had been prescribed to prevent the side effects of other medications that I stopped taking them. That, and the fact they had not solved my core issue, which still persisted.

I believe that if we can change the social mindset, it will lessen the misunderstanding and ensure that when we speak of mental illness (which is used far more than it should in my view) it focuses on the mind. Often, I hear on the news how someone with mental illness did something horrible, only to then find out they had been diagnosed with depression or bipolar disorder. It gives the wrong impression and the stigma associated with it alienates people who suffer, leaving those who really need more human contact isolated.

It is this alienation that creates a pattern that is very difficult to escape when you do suffer from social anxiety, panic attacks and suchlike. In order to desensitise these feelings and our incorrect programming, we need more opportunities to interact. We just need to do it safely, and with great understanding and patience. But so far, all I can see is society going the other way.

The stigma about mental health is worse than ever before, with bigotry and misconceptions that help nobody. This needs to change, and change quickly, with the aid of education in society, business and especially the media, who peddle and disseminate these ideas with soundbites that misrepresent people. I hope to help this in some way, and I hope we all do.

What makes this more socially difficult for men is the common perception of masculinity. Built in from a young age is the idea that boys should be strong and independent. With this perception it is difficult for a man to open up and say he's struggling. I have found it is very difficult to open up about it. No man wants to appear weak and talk about the invisible illness that they struggle with every day.

So the problem with mental health today is that we still do not understand it, or more how to talk about it, so instead we use the phrase inappropriately. We do not understand what it means to suffer from it because everyone's tolerance to life is different, yet we still make assumptions and lump sufferers together. Furthermore, this is not a new problem, as conditions like depression, anxiety, and bipolar disorders have been recognised for over a hundred years, albeit by different names.

We should be learning from our history, and putting in place preventive measures to stop the causes, aid understanding. This should have started yesterday, but could start today.

Only society can do this, we have the technology, the money, and the people, What we do not have or lacking is the will.

Chapter 11

Can I help someone who suffers?

First of all, I want to thank anyone who can see someone suffering, and actually wants to get into the dirt to help. There is no quick fix, and it's complicated to get to the underlying issues. A psychotherapist is the best option to start with. Personally I do not see much difference between a councillor and a psychotherapist, but it may depend on the level of help a person needs and the experience of the therapist. However, the demand is very high, and so are the waiting lists for NHS treatment in mental health. So to help is to try to prevent someone from getting worse. This in itself is not easy.

The main problem with giving suggestions is that no method fixes all.

This is why I cannot offer specific advice, as neither of us can afford to get it wrong for the sake of the person suffering. As I have said, sometimes the best of intentions can backfire and do more harm than good. So treading slowly, carefully, but always forward is what I would suggest. It also very much depends on how the person suffering is related to you. Trust is a huge part of helping someone.

Without trust, no intervention will help, and instead it will undoubtedly harm. Finally, it is important not to judge. You should expect to hear things you'd rather not have heard, but expressing these is also important. You simply cannot put yourself in their shoes and find a way for them. This is vital, in my opinion, to help them. I looked for many years for someone to help me, direct me, or even push me. And although people did, they pushed me the wrong way every time and because of that, I am broken. Healing one's mind must come from within the sufferer. If they are not wanting to be helped, or change, it will not happen. So please be sure it's what they want. I can assure you that watching someone suffer and being helpless while trying very hard to help will wear you down to the point of giving up. This also helps nobody.

What I can do is give you a story of what I have done to help someone very dear to me. They have suffered in the past few months, although it could be said they have actually been suffering for several years. In the past few months, however, it has become unbearable for them. With trust, time and, more importantly, listening carefully, I was able to discover two major issues relating to their panic attacks. This is after seeking medical advice and tests, to ensure it was not any type of physical issue or deficiency. It should be suggested that this is the first thing to do: have them see their doctor. In this case, it came down to two issues: abandonment and social anxiety. These led to panic attacks and becoming so stressed it resulted in not eating for fear of being sick.

It is worth stressing at this point that interactions with someone suffering from social anxiety can be very hard. You do want them to go out. They do need to desensitise to social environments, but you also need to be mindful of who they interact with. It's a balance that needs one hand under each scale. And this, in a nutshell, is what is involved in helping them. Moving forward at a rate that is best for all concerned, and providing a cushion to catch them should they need it.

In this case, a sense of abandonment had always been in the background, and although as time passed the person had evidence that further abandonment is unlikely, this didn't, as might be expected, desensitise them. I do not understand why, though even in my case, thirty years on and still surviving, you might think my vulnerabilities should have decreased, but they haven't. Speed up to this year and after feeling unwell due to excess of a non-alcoholic drink, this triggered something in this person. They had not been physically sick, but did feel very unwell for a good few days. From here on in, eating became a concern to them. They didn't want to feel unwell again so didn't want to eat. This pattern led to them feeling unwell because they hadn't eaten, and so the cycle began. The panicking would start when they needed to go out, because they worried about feeling unwell while out of the house. This caused an issue because we had to determine whether the feeling of being unwell was due to anxiety or due to being hungry. It would be too simplistic to assume one cause without ruling the other out. Otherwise, we would be misdiagnosing the cause and worsening the situation.

So we started by making sure food had been eaten, with three meals per day: a cooked breakfast, lunch and dinner. When you do not eat for a few days, adding into the equation your metabolism and any exercise undertaken, the tummy shrinks while also gaining air. Then when you eat, the tummy expands and air can get trapped. This can be very uncomfortable and can lead to the feeling of being unwell, which in turn can restart the cycle. To prevent this we went for a walk around the block after we had eaten, after a few trips up and down stairs while breathing in through our nose and out through our mouths in a timely fashion. This helps digest food, shakes air to the top of the tummy and extinguishes it, one way or another. So long as any trapped air can get out, it will relieve the feeling of bloating and being uncomfortable.

Once we had done this for two days, we then focused on two main elements, social anxiety and desensitising, as well as looking at the bigger picture. It is a good idea to put things into perspective. To do this you basically note the successes, such as eating, and bring into focus the fact they survived the ordeal they had anxiety about to start with. Praise for successful small steps brings about confidence and trust, which are very important.

This is probably one of the hardest parts for both parties as it requires time. In my case, it was three steps forward, one step back. But you have to go with the flow, and trust in each other, all the time listening and reassuring. Try to establish a routine and keep to it. If you need support from places of work or education, then explain what is happening, and how you are helping. Ask for their support to allow this to continue within their work or school environment. In this case, I met the person for lunch every day for two weeks and took them away from a stressful environment for a respite while ensuring they were eating. I remained with them until it was time to go back, but with the reassurance that should they start to panic and feel unable to keep it under control, I would come back and either sit with them or take them home. What is important here is that they try.

The biggest setback people suffering in this way, and anyone helping them, can have is not trying. This is why a routine is such a good idea. Yes, you may take a step backwards, but keep to the routine. This is how you desensitise and re-programme. Over time it will sidestep the pathway to panic. Having that constant reassurance was important. Knowing they are not alone, and trusting someone who will not let them down is huge, and I cannot tell you how incredibly important it is.

Once it is established that the thought of, or the feeling of, being unwell is not down to a lack of food, we can focus more on the association of panic itself. As I have explained, the younger the person is, the easier it is to create pathways in the brain that associate sickness or pain with panic. So to re-programme this, we need to support situations that have in the past, or are likely to in future, bring about this vulnerability. One of the fastest ways I have found to do this is by keeping them preoccupied. I needed them to be thinking of something else before, and during, the situation or environment that is likely to cause distress. My way of keeping them occupied was a mix of learning new, fun, and focusing on future events. These future events are not distant, but just 30-minute slots. This and talking about what will happen removes the cycle of panic because they focus on other things. Once they have achieved the goal of being in social environments, they draw new pathways. So it is important to champion successes so the path from going out, getting to a required event, and leaving it, bypasses the thought process of panic, distress and the symptoms that come with it. We had to do this several times over three months before it became normal.

Then comes the task of removing the support, as you cannot allow them to rely on you indefinitely. However much someone may want that, it's not good for them. I know it feels good to be needed. It fills the heart to be wanted and as such I know it's hard to let go. But I assure you, slowly does it, let go you must for their sake. In this instance,

I slowly stopped meeting them for lunch. I gave requests for them to go out, small and steady every time. This went on for a short time before they no longer needed me, their confidence returned and the path forward was again opening up. Big events may require some support, at least now and then, so please be there for them in those cases.

This is what I did to help someone who had no physical illness. I do not want to say everything I did would work for everyone, but the core principles are trust, support and listening, always without judgement. Some notes from my own experiences are that younger people and those with a low IQ will struggle to articulate and understand their feelings. It is best not to lead, but to follow in these cases. Ask as many questions as you can, and perhaps word it differently to ensure the answer you are getting has a high degree of accuracy. It can be difficult, but is well worth the extra time in the end.

I would finally suggest you only attempt it if you have time, and patience. Remember they must do the hard work, and this in itself may take longer than you expect. You are important too, as is your own mental health.

Chapter 12

What are these ripples.

Over time, I've developed my idea of a ripple. Ripples have far-reaching, and long lasting, effects. Here, I'll explain why I speak of them the way I do.

Imagine throwing a stone into a lake, and seeing the splash. The splash is the immediate effect, a reaction of a force hitting the water. This I consider the knee-jerk reaction. What follows are the small waves from the splash in every direction, with its force then fading back into the calmness of the lake. Now, consider the lake to be a shallow puddle; the puddle is the world and every one of us is causing a splash every time we take a step, or say a word. And the effect of the step or a word comes with a knee-jerk reaction, and the waves, or ripples, that follow.

These ripples of course interact with each other, but not only on the surface of the water, where we can see them, but also underneath. As with any interaction, there are positive and negative effects. Life is about either ignoring the negatives, or using them by turning them into positives. I guess it depends on the ripple whether it will be easy to change for the good, or to ignore. But the bigger picture shows that although something might be a negative for you, it could be a positive for someone else. And that, right there, is life.

In either case, the ripples drive life, not just for you but for everyone, and if you don't cause ripples then you are not contributing to what could be. My ripples led me to many places, helping many people and bringing up an amazing girl on my own. She is now creating her own ripples and affecting the lives of many others too.

This is to say to you, and to reinforce the truth, that *you* are important. No matter the crap you have to live through, however tough life is and how low you get, the ripples you make do and will always have an impact on others. But remember others' ripples also impact you. What goes around comes around. So be honest and true to yourself, and trust that the steps you are taking are important, and so are you.

It is also true to say that not all impacts are good for everyone. I make ripples that upset people, and I can tell you many more ripples made by other people that affect me are not positive in any way, shape or form. In fact they bring me to the brink, daily. Negative ripples include rudeness, inconsiderateness and selfishness, and people do this all the time. It may not be on purpose; it might just be that they are also having a bad day. But this is the way of the ripple: it can lift you or capsize you, all in the blink of an eye.

Yet negative ripples are how we learn, it's an experience we have to deal with. Every ripple is a lesson that each and every one of us must go through as part of our journey in life. So yes, they can be tough and can kick us further down, even when we thought we had reached rock bottom. The lesson comes from getting back up, and when we see a possible recurrence in our future, we sidestep it.

This is the nature of a ripple, and to create ripples we have to live.

Chapter 13

Life at 50.

During the two years of Covid-19 lockdowns I did a lot of experiments to clarify, yet again, that food is not a cause of my episodes. This is because whenever I move house, which I do often because of my own insecurities about being in one place for too long, I register with a new doctor and they seem too busy to read notes, and so ask the same questions and give the same advice over and over again. I understand they are busy, even more so in these times, but as a sufferer of an invisible condition that is not truly understood, even by myself, the need to improve myself is so very important.

It is an interesting exercise to experiment and analyse the results. In a way, as I have said before, it's really your own CBT. When you're testing yourself, and when you get good results, you are desensitising the emotion, or trigger, from the physical aspects of the condition. Still, that does not mean you're fixed.

I'll have high hopes for a couple of days, but then crash and burn on the third. I have been testing myself and pushing myself all my life. I have never really given up and I really do want to improve my standard of life, but even at this age I have been unable to find precise triggers, other than the broad range of 'vulnerability'. So I still struggle, and it can still be frustrating. But I just think of the ripples I created, and those of my daughter. And now I hope this book will also help people, causing even more ripples.

Having confirmed from my experiments that food is not the cause of my episodes, I have identified an issue about my environment. Although I knew this already, it was clearly noticeable during my last couple of bad episodes that lasted weeks, rather than days. Explaining this to my new doctors' surgery, I discovered that on my notes, especially for the past ten-plus years, there is no mention that I suffer from PTSD. I was both a little shocked and strangely intrigued.

I did not see a regular GP; I spoke to a mental health professional and when I explained my situation and symptoms it was clear to him I had PTSD, but as a nurse he was unable to diagnose me. So I was referred to a specialist unit for a diagnosis. I had a letter back from this specialist unit saying they would not see me because they also could not give a diagnosis. They then suggested another part of the health system for help. So I called them and guess what! They also do not give diagnoses.

I think despite the buzz word that is mental health at the moment, the reality on the ground is that the system is far from perfect. You have to fight, and never give up or lose hope, because all the time you're paddling against the current, taking more steps back than forward, you are creating larger ripples and they do help, support and give promise to others.

I wanted to add this to the book to explain that you can never ask enough questions when you have a mental health condition where the causes are invisible, but the symptoms are very visible. Clearly having a diagnosis is important to finding a manageable solution. Without one, not only can you not help yourself, but the GP cannot help you either. In my experience, having been misdiagnosed myself, it could mean being prescribed the wrong medication, which only makes everything worse.

I think this demonstrates the need to keep up to date with current and past medical records, letters, etc. I feel it will save time and frustration when you are looking for self-improvement, and the less you have to rely on others, such as in my case, the better it is for everyone.

Now in my fiftieth year, and looking back on my own life I wish I had had more help, more support and much less medication. I honestly feel I lost ten to fifteen years of my life because I was on the wrong medication, with the side effects masking my real core issues. It is so important to ask questions, so important to understand what is happening to you, and what is being said to you. Having a close friend or family member with you at appointments makes all the difference, so never be afraid to ask for help from those closest to you.

Looking back to my life as a young man and looking at young people today, I think we have a long way to go. I believe steps in the right direction have been made, but I consider these just steps, not the strides needed. We must help our young people dealing with any type of mental illness. We need to explain both to those suffering, and those who are not, especially boys, that it is not a weakness to ask for help.

It is not a weakness to open up and explain. It is strength that allows you to do this. Being afraid is a natural feeling, but so is curiosity and finding solutions. Any type of learning starts with asking questions. Do not put it off, start asking and do not stop until you are content with the answers.

And remember, your life is important, whether you are alone, or in a crowd with people around. You exist for a reason, but you need to keep healthy to find out what it is. Only then will you look around you with a new perspective on people, life and real purpose. It's not all about being fixed. I am still not fixed, I am not a happy ending to my book, and paddling to stay afloat, just like others. But I have found purpose, and I am important, just like you!

Final Thoughts

I think it's important that we understand how we are placed in the world. You are important, everything about you is important and if like me, or somebody you know, you struggle with everyday routines because of mental illness, you are just as important as everyone else. I have learnt that despite the struggles you will continue to grow from the experiences you live through.

These struggles shape your personality and natural abilities and although this may not be what you expected, it's important you try to understand it, manage it and learn to live with it as best you can. I know this is easy to say, and I understand the many levels of frustration that go along with this. But to realise there is a bigger picture means everything.

Though these struggles can, and do, define us, what is so often not realised is the people we touch along the way, most of the time without realising it, or even meaning to. This influence has a lasting effect on others. Those of us who suffer with mental illnesses do live marked lives, but these lives are not worthless! They have a purpose and a reason, even if we do not always understand what those are. As well as creating our own ripples, other ripples influence us too.

My perspective is very different from that of most people because of my experience, and has a profound effect that helps shape, or move, others. But because mental illnesses have a negative stigma attached, society is missing out on realising these effects. Mental health and mental illness are buzzwords. The government talks about them a lot, but they are not actually improving the situation. They think that if they use those words enough it makes it sound like they are doing something about it.

As you have read throughout this book, my case is complicated and has provided doctors, as well as therapists, with a few curveballs, hence the missed and simply incorrect diagnoses. To a degree blame can be assigned, but as the emotions flow and triggers are fired, it really is only down to us to find and manage the symptoms, or, even better, understand and then beat the causes.

I hope that reading about my experiences and the journey I have taken to date, shines some light for others. I want to show those suffering, and those who see others suffer, the importance of self-worth, even in the darkest times. To show that it is worth pushing on, not giving up, and speaking honestly to those closest to you about the struggle. There is a bigger picture, and we are all an important part of it.

What happened to me is not common, but mental health is all about the uncommon and because we all have different breaking points, strengths and limits of coping all in different areas of our very being, the pain, anguish, isolation and just plain misery we have to go through are different. So what might come easy for me, will be difficult for another, and vice versa!

As a society, and as individuals, we need to understand that mental health is not just a phrase. It's not a box you can lump everyone into. Mental health is not like an umbrella with hundreds of people under it suffering in the same way, but many umbrellas with many people under them suffering in very different ways.

My feeling of what's most important, what I believe to be the answer is how we bring up our children, and the environment we bring them up in.

The foundation of many mental illnesses starts from the late stages of development within the womb. Also worth noting my distinction between mental and physical illnesses of the mind. Whether you believe it's genetics or not, it still comes down to how we can help future generations cope with life, and its challenges, without many of these conditions suffered today. With the number of cases of young people suffering a mental illness, increasing year after year the knock-on effect means the longer we wait to act, the longer it will take to correct.

The consequence of doing nothing, or using sticking plasters, is the cost both financially and socially, will become unmanageable. Leading to higher suicides, drug and alcohol abuse, and further unintended and unforeseen consequences.

We have to act now, and together.

Perhaps this book will highlight some of these ways. Perhaps it demonstrates the complexities of a young person's case that can generate fresh new ideas on how to resolve them. I do hope this book can help at least one person live a better life.

But more than anything, I hope that everybody young, or old, who suffers from a mental illness understands the importance of living. You are worthwhile, and important, not just to those closest, but to the many seen and unseen as well as society in general.

You are not alone and you deserve to be listened to and be heard.

Made in the USA
Monee, IL
04 November 2026

67374714R00069